Using a Clay Machine

1. Change the Number Setting

The knob on the left side of the Clay Machine controls the width between the rollers.

Positions are marked by numbers 1 to 9 depending on the brand of the machine. Pull out knob and turn to change the number.

2. Guide the Clay

Keep the sheet of clay smooth and prevent it from doubling over on itself as it comes through the Clay Machine by guiding it with your hand.

Gently use your palm to pull the clay toward you.

3. Clean the Rollers

To keep the Clay Machine and clay clean, run a paper towel between the rollers, and wipe the machine and rollers on the top and underneath.

This step is especially important between colors.

Condition Polymer Clay to Make It Soft

This is the best method to use for 'new' clay that is fairly soft when you open the package.

Remember to always 'condition' the clay as it will work better and the polymers will adhere together better.

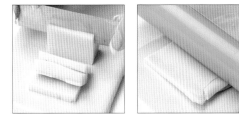

1. Slice the clay slightly thicker than the thickest setting on the Clay Machine.

2. Flatten the clay slab with an acrylic brayer.

3. Run the clay slab through your Clay Machine on the thickest setting until smooth and elastic, folding clay after each pass through the machine. Keep fold at the side or bottom to prevent trapped air bubbles between the layers.

For best results, slightly flatten chunks of clay with a roller or your hand before running them through the Clay Machine.

Fold the flattened slab piece in half. Repeat until the clay is uniformly warm and soft (10-12 times).

How to Dye and Color Polymer Clay

Liquid Dyes & Paints

Work over a craft sheet, wear protective gloves and have paper towels on hand.

1. Squirt a small amount of the desired ink onto the center of a conditioned sheet of clay. (If using Alcohol Inks, let the ink dry completely before proceeding to the next step.).

2. Fold the inked sheet and run it through the Clay Machine on the widest setting, the folded edge first. (This may be messy, wipe ink and re-incorporate ink into the clay.)

3. Repeat this step until the ink is evenly dispersed in the clay.

TIP: Dye makes the clay very sticky. Allowing the clay to rest and firm up for 1 hour makes it easier to handle.

Colors & Embossing Powders

Work over a craft sheet, wear protective gloves and have paper towels on hand.

1. Spoon about $\frac{1}{2}$ tsp. of Embossing Powder onto the center of a conditioned sheet of clay.

2. Fold the sheet in half, enclosing the powder inside the clay.

3. Run clay through the Clay Machine, fold first. Repeat this step, adding powder as needed to achieve the shade you desire.

TIP: Excessive powder may compromise the structure of your piece. Add more clay if the mixture begins to crumble.

Baked clays will differ in appearance, so adjust the clay-to-powder ratio accordingly. Make a set of color chips for reference.

Perfect 'To Dye For' Bracelet

by Debbie Tlach

Easy, pretty and fun to wear!

SIZE: Bracelet 8"; Ovals ¾" x 1⅛"

MATERIALS:

Polymer Clay:
Kato Polyclay (White, Black) • Liquid Polyclay

Dye Supplies:
Ranger (*To Dye For* Ink sets - Primary, Hot
• Perfect Pearls - Perfect Gold, Perfect Bronze, Kiwi, Forever Red, Forever Blue)

Materials:
Hampton Art Stamps Letter stamps • *Lara's Crafts* Annealed wire 20 gauge • Bracelet closure clasp

Tools:
Makin's (Professional Ultimate Clay Machine; Oval Cutter Set) • *Ranger* (Inkssentials Non-Stick Craft Sheet, Heat it Craft Tool; Perfect Pearls large brush) • *3M* Fine grit sanding pad • Round-nose pliers • Flat-nose pliers • Wire cutters

INSTRUCTIONS:

Prep: Condition and roll out a slab of Black clay on the 3rd largest setting on the Clay Machine.
Stamp: Stamp into the clay with a letters stamp.

1. Use your finger to apply various colors of the Perfect Pearls to the raised part of the stamped clay. Flatten gently with an acrylic roller, and then roll embellished clay through the Clay Machine on the 3rd thickest setting.
2. Using a medium sized oval cutter, cut 5-6 ovals from Black clay from the sheet (depending on desired circumference of bracelet). Cut 6" of wire for each oval. Gently flip the ovals over and press the wire lengthwise into the pieces.
3. Condition and roll out a slab of White clay on the widest setting. Stamp into the clay with the letters stamp. Cut 5-6 White ovals. Brush Liquid Polyclay on Black ovals and gently place White ovals on top, sandwiching the wire in between the ovals. Bake clay following manufacturer's directions. Let cool. Lightly sand enough to remove the shine from the White top and sides of the ovals.
4. Tape the wire pieces of 1 oval to the craft sheet to stabilize the piece. Squeeze a small amount of Blue and Green To Dye For ink colors onto the Craft Sheet. Using the brush and some water, pool To Dye For colors onto the White oval letting the colors run down the sides as well. Heat with the Heat it Tool adding more To Dye For and water as needed. Let cool briefly. Sand the edges, sides, and top just enough to lighten the raised areas. • Repeat using the following color combinations: Yellow & Blue, Yellow & Orange, Orange & Red, Red & Magenta and Magenta & Yellow if there is a 6th piece.
5. Use wire tools to attach the oval pieces to each other. Finish by adding a closure clasp to the ends.

Each stone animal was created using a different shade of Distress Embossing Powder, then tinted with Alcohol Inks. The possibilities are endless!

Antiquities Embossing Powder

Cement · Tanzanite · AN Cobalt · AN Verdigris · Topiary · Christmas Tree

'Stone' Animals

by Leslie Blackford
Unique animals are great starters.

MATERIALS:
Polymer Clay: Translucent *Kato* Polyclay

1. Sculpting the animal: Create the body. Shape the arms and legs. Shape the head and add the ears.
2. Insert seed beads into the head for the eyes.

 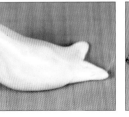 

Dye Supplies: *Ranger* (Adirondack Alcohol Inks - Espresso, Lettuce, Mushroom, Oregano, Pesto; Distress Embossing powders - Weathered Wood, Peeled Paint, Old Paper; Embossing Antiquities - Topiary, Rose Quartz, Cobalt)
Materials: Seed beads
Tools: Sculpting & Carving tools • Non-stick Craft Sheet

INSTRUCTIONS:
Use the sample chart to select color of the stone animal that you would like to create. • Mix ¼ block of Translucent clay with ¼ tsp of the embossing powder that you have selected. Run the clay and powder through the Clay Machine several times until the powder and clay have mixed evenly.

3. Carve the details into the body of the animal with a sharp needle tool. Carve more detail into the face and around the eyes. Smooth out all fingerprints and smudges on the surface. Bake at 275° for 20 minutes. While the animal is still hot from the oven. drop it directly into a bowl of ice water making sure that the piece is completely submerged.
4. Aging the animal: Dry the animal off, making sure no water is left in the carved lines. Use a soft brush to apply Espresso Ink onto the surface of the animal. Let the ink bleed into the cracks of the carvings. Wipe away all excess ink from the animal, leaving the Espresso ink mainly in the carved places of the animal. Sand and buff animal if desired.
5. Drill a hole and attach to a cord or chain for an original work of art.

Rust · California Stucco · Ocher · Rose Quartz · Terra Cotta · Chinese Red · Claret

Embossing Powders and Clay

by Donna Kato

Mixing embossing powder into polymer clay creates simple stone imitations!

Mix Embossing powder into Translucent clay and the "stone" takes on the color of the powder; the more powder you mix in, the more intense the color.

This necklace features two beautiful 'stones' made by mixing powder into Translucent and one stone made by mixing powder into Black clay.

'Three Stones' Embossing Powder Necklace

MATERIALS:
Polymer Clay:
Kato Polyclay (Black, Translucent)
Dye Supplies:
Ranger Embossing Antiquities - Claret, Rust, Weathered White, Verdigris
Materials: Buna cord • 'O' rings • Super glue
Tools:
Clay Machine • Knitting needle or bamboo skewer • Needle tool
INSTRUCTIONS:
Mix Powder into Polyclay:
Roll a sheet of conditioned clay through the thickest setting of the Clay Machine. Spoon powder onto the clay. Fold the clay over, encasing the powder. Place the fold on the rollers. Roll clay. Continue folding and rolling until the powder is integrated into the clay. It's best to work gradually, adding and mixing powder as you go until you have achieved the color intensity you desire.

Verdigris Mix: Spread powder on a sheet of Translucent clay. The piece directly below shows what the clay/powder mix looks like. The piece to the right came from the same mixture – it has been baked. The color in raw clay is often not the same as cured clay.
Rose Mix: Claret and Rust are mixed into Translucent clay.
Black Mix: Weathered White embossing powder is mixed into Black clay. Once the White powder is cured, it will form White bits on the surface.
Verdigris Bead: 4. Roll clay into a cylinder (left). Round into a flattened barrel shape (center). Flatten further between the palms of your hands (right). Shape the remaining 2 beads. Drilling Bead Holes: Arrange the beads as they will be strung. The top bead is where the cord end will be secured and where the cord itself will also be strung through. My top bead is the verdigris colored bead.
5. With a needle tool at an angle, drill through the bead. Enlarge the hole by drilling through again with a knitting needle or bamboo skewer. The diameter of this tool should be the same size as the diameter of the cord or a bit larger.

Archival & Archival Brights Reinkers

Coffee Sepia Russet Crimson Tangerine Banana Mustard Olive Emerald Aqua

6. With the needle tool, drill ¼" into the bead, but not through the bead. The knitting needle is in the previously drilled hole to show the relative placement and the angle at which the second hole is drilled. • **7.** Enlarge the hole with the knitting needle. Cord and Stringing: Cut buna cord long enough to wrap around your head, plus 8". • **8.** Glue an 'O' ring onto the end of the cord. Snip the cord right up to the ring. • **9.** Referring to photo for placement, string beads on a cord with the glued 'O' ring on the end. There are no 'O' rings snugged up against the Verdigris bead so the cord slides freely. • **10**. Securing the cord end: Place an 'O' RING on the cord. Glue the cord into the hole using Super glue.

Archival & Archival Brights Reinkers

Library Green · True Blue · Teal · Berry Purple · Cobalt · Grape · Jet Black · Plum · Maroon · Carnation

Cracker Earrings

by Debbie Tlach
This project came from the pure joy of artists being together.
I was talking about the product Mold n' Pour, and how it can be baked with clay in the mold
I molded just a simple object – a cheese cracker. Try it... it's fun!

SIZE: 1" x 1"
MATERIALS:
Polymer Clay:: *Kato* Polyclay (White, Orange, Yellow, Turquoise)
Materials: 2 ear wires • 22 gauge Silver wire • 1 small cheese cracker
Tools: *Ranger* Mold n' Pour (White, Purple) • Flat-nose pliers • Round-nose pliers • Wire cutters • Non-stick Craft Sheet

1. Mix equal parts of the White and Purple Mold n' Pour material following the manufacturer's directions. • **2.** Press a cheese cracker into the Mold n' Pour. Let the mold set up, 7-8 minutes. Pop cracker out of the mold and discard. • **3.** Mix 4 parts White clay with 2 parts Orange, 1 part Yellow and a pinch of Turquoise. If the Orange is too bright, add small amounts of Turquoise until the correct hue is achieved. Divide clay in half and add a little more Turquoise to make it slightly darker. Marble the 2 shades of clay together by twisting and rolling a few times. Press a small amount of clay into the mold filling it and smoothing the back.

4. Cut a 2" piece of wire. Using flat-nose pliers, bend into a 45° angle. Using round-nose pliers, form a loop with the wire. Holding the loop with flat-nose pliers, wrap wire around the bottom of loop 2 times. Cut off excess wire. Bend the tail end in several places.
TIP: Embedding this end in the clay will ensure that the wire will not pull out of the clay.

5. Place the wire so that the loop protrudes over the corner edge of the clay in the mold.
6. Place a small patch of clay over the wire and gently press to embed the wire in the clay. Smooth if desired. • **7.** Bake the mold and clay at 275° for 20 minutes. Let cool and pop out of the mold. Attach ear wire.

Swirl Art Star Earrings

Colorful earring are bright, fun shapes and great to make.

SIZE:
Stars 1⅜" x 1⅜"
Rectangles ¾" x 1½"
MATERIALS:
Polymer Clay: *Kato* (Liquid Polyclay, White Polyclay)
Dye Supplies: *Ranger Adirondack* Alcohol Inks - Butterscotch, Red Pepper, Stream, Wild Plum, Lettuce & Terra Cotta
Materials: Scrap cardstock • *Junkitz* Ringz ¼" jump rings • Antique Brass • ⅛" Bronze eyelets • Ear wires • Crazy Glue or eyelet tools • 1-2 wooden 2¼" finials • Protective goggles and gloves
Tools: *Ranger* Inkssentials Non-Stick Craft Sheet • *Makin's* (Star Cutter Set; Clay Machine) • *Natural Science Ind. Ltd* Swirl 'N' Spin
INSTRUCTIONS:
1. Cut a piece of cardstock to fit into the turntable brackets of the Swirl 'N' Spin. Working over the Craft Sheet, condition and roll out White clay on the 6th largest setting on the Clay Machine. Cut the sheet of clay to fit on top of the cardstock, and insert into Swirl 'N' Spin holding brackets.
2. Wear protective goggles and gloves. Turn Swirl 'N' Spin on. Squeeze drops of all the Alcohol Ink colors randomly over the spinning clay. Turn Swirl 'N' Spin off. If you are happy with the pattern, allow the ink to dry for 2-5 minutes. Carefully remove clay-covered cardstock. If you are not happy, turn it back on and apply more colors to the clay. You can add color to a previously colored area because the Alcohol Ink will re-wet itself.
3. Carefully cut 2 stars from the inked clay using the large star cutter. Following manufacturer's instructions, bake each star on top of the finial to achieve the curved shape. Let the shape cool completely on top of the finial.
4. Punch a ⅛" hole in the star.
5. Leave uncoated or, for a slightly muted watercolor effect, coat with Liquid Polyclay, then rebake on finial.
6. Set or glue eyelet. Attach 2 jump rings and an ear wire to each earring.

Swirl Art on Clay

by Debbie Tlach

Vibrant colors, dynamic colors, spectacular patterns! Create fun and interesting designs in just minutes with Adirondack Alcohol Inks and Polymer Clay. I love creating colorful jewelry and earrings, but you can decorate almost anything.

1. While the machine is spinning, drip Alcohol Ink colors onto the clay.

2. Bake each star on top of a round wood finial to achieve a curved shape.

Tips and Techniques

1. Always wear protective goggles when using the Swirl 'N' Spin. Wear old clothes when working with inks. Wear protective gloves whenever you use Alcohol Ink to prevent staining your hands. If you do get stained, use a pumice soap to remove ink.

2. Roll clay almost paper thin by sandwiching between 2 sheets of waxed paper, bake the clay sheet & add ink. Use various paper punches to cut shapes.

Add a layer of polish with Liquid Polyclay, to create stunning jewelry.

1. Condition ½ pkg of Pearl *Kato* Polyclay and ½ pkg of Translucent Clay. Mix the 2 together. Kato metallic clays are so infused with mica particles this technique works best when mixing in equal parts of metallic clays with Translucent. Roll the clay into a large sheet on the thickest setting of the Clay Machine. Cut the sheet in half.

2. Wear gloves. This is very messy. The dye is water based so cleanup with soap and water is a snap! Squirt a good amount of Magenta To Dye For on ½ of the clay sheet. Squirt Orange on the other sheet.
3. This dye will not dry on the clay, so fold the sheet in half and run through the Clay Machine.

4. The dye will squirt out of the top. Just keep swiping the ink up and smear it back on the clay. Continue folding the clay and rolling it through the Clay Machine until the dye is completely incorporated into the clay. Follow the same procedure to incorporate the Orange To Dye For into the other half of the Pearl/Translucent clay. The dye makes the clay very sticky. Allowing the clay to rest and firm up for 1 hour makes it easier to handle. • **5.** Form each color into a rectangle 2" x 3". • **6.** Cut each rectangle in half diagonally to form 2 right triangles. Stack like-color triangles on top of each other. • **7.** Join the diagonal edge, offsetting the triangles slightly so that the corners do not exactly meet. Trim the tips that hang above and below to reform the sheet into a rectangle. You must do this if you wish to have areas of the graded color clay sheet that are the 2 colors you began with. If the colors meet exactly, you will have a sheet that is entirely graded. • **8.** Roll the sheets through the Clay Machine set on the thickest setting, making sure both colors are touching the roller of the pasta machine. Fold the 2 color sheet in half, matching same-color edge on same-color edge.

9. Place the fold against the rollers of the Clay Machine and roll through the Clay Machine. Placing the folded edge against the Clay Machine roller insures that you don't trap air into the blend. • **10.** The clay will tend to spread out across the rollers of the Clay Machine causing the blend to widen. To keep this from happening, use the sides of the Clay Machine to wedge the clay. Turn the entire blend each time you roll it through so that the magenta side of the blend is against the side and then the next pass through the machine the Orange side is against the side. Repeat until the sheet is fully blended and there are no streaks. This may take approximately 20 times through the Clay Machine. • **11.** Place the clay sheet on a small ceramic tile and allow the clay to rest for 30 minutes to firm up. To keep the ceramic tile from moving, adhere it to your work surface with double-sided tape. • **12.** Mist the rubber stamp with water. • **13.** Press stamp firmly into the clay.

14. Carefully shave off the raised portion of the clay. Sometimes it is helpful to bend the blade slightly and shave off smaller areas at a time. Continue to shave all the raised areas until the remaining sheet is smooth. • **15.** Smooth the surface of the clay to a glass-like finish using an acrylic rod. • **16.** Cut a 2" oval of clay. Remove the excess clay. • **17.** Bend the clay blade and cut ½ of the oval into a moon shape. • **18.** Bend the clay blade the other direction to make the second moon shape.

Pearl & Translucent Clay with 'To Dye For' Inks

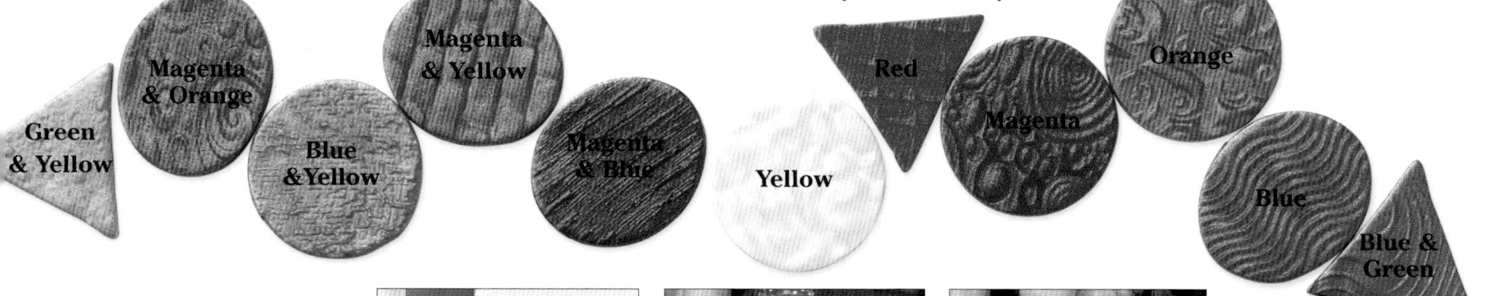

(Sample chips labeled around the top and right border:)

Green & Yellow · Magenta & Orange · Blue & Yellow · Magenta & Yellow · Magenta & Blue · Yellow · Red · Magenta · Orange · Blue · Blue & Green · Orange & Yellow · Red & Yellow · Green · Red & Orange

Amazing Colors

by Judy Belcher

I have always loved metallic clays and the interesting effects you can get with them.

Now, you can have that same effect in vibrant colors without losing any of the translucency of metallic clays. 'To Dye For' colors are translucent and they color the clay beautifully.

Many of you may recognize the Skinner Blend polymer clay technique, named for Judith Skinner who developed it.

'To DYE For' Moon Earrings

SIZE: 1" x 2⅛"

MATERIALS:

Polymer Clay: *Kato* Polyclay (Black, Pearl, Translucent)

Dye Supplies: *Ranger* (Black Soot Distress Embossing Powder; *To Dye For* - Magenta, Orange)

Materials: Glass Christmas ornament or light bulb • *JudiKins* Relish Background rubber stamp • Jump rings • Earring findings

Tools: *Ranger* Rub-It Scrub It pad • Clay Machine • Clay Blade • *Ateco* 2" Oval Cutter • Chain-nose pliers

INSTRUCTIONS:

Earring Assembly:
Using chain-nose pliers, open a jump ring by twisting it open to the side. Place the jump ring through the Black moon-shaped earring and then the colored piece. Attach an earring finding and close the jump ring.

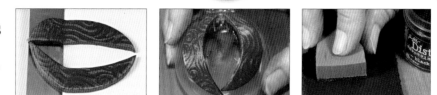

19. Using the clay blade, carefully slice under each moon shape to remove from the tile. • **20.** For a nice curve, place the moon shaped clay on a glass Christmas bulb or light bulb. Bake for 20 minutes at 275°. • **21.** Condition ⅓ bar Black clay. Sprinkle ½ teaspoon Black Distress Embossing Powder over the clay. Press powder into clay with Rubit Scrubit pad. Roll the Black clay on a medium setting.

22. Cut ovals as before and make moon shapes. • **23.** While the Black moon shapes are on the Christmas bulb, gently texture the surface with a Rubit Scrubit pad. This will make the moon shapes slightly larger and give them an interesting texture. Bake for 20 minutes at 275°. When the earrings are cool remove them from the bulb. • **24.** Drill a hole near the top of each of the moon shapes using a ⅛" drill bit in a hand drill or Dremel.

Apply the techniques explained in 'To Dye For' Moon Earrings to make this exquisite necklace. Simply vary the inks and rubber stamps to create your own exciting line of accessories.

Mushroom Oregano Pesto Lettuce Meadow

Ir-Resist-ible Gift Tags

by Judy Belcher

Everyone likes to give and receive gifts and the techniques used on these tags can easily be translated to any scrapbook page.

The fun began when Debbie, Marcia and I began to play with the leftover tags. The sample tags are all a group effort and examples of what can happen when artists gather together and share!

SIZE: 1¾" x 3¾"

MATERIALS:

Polymer Clay: *Kato* (Liquid Medium; White Polyclay)

Dye Supplies: *Ranger* (Cut N' Dry Foam; Adirondack Acrylics - Butterscotch, Cranberry)

Materials: Rubber stamps (*JudiKins* Circles in Circles Background, Mod Pattern Cube) • Cardstock (Yellow, Red) • Fibers • Alcohol • Terrifically Tacky Tape

Tools: *Ranger* (Inky Roller, Non-stick Craft Sheet) • *Sizzix* tags and circle die cuts • *Ateco* Circle cutters (1", 2") • Spray water bottle

Tips and Techniques

This is a quick and easy way to do a resist method on either a gift tag or a whole sheet of scrapbook paper.

Terrifically Tacky Tape is the best product I have found to adhere polymer clay to paper.

1. Die-cut a tag from Yellow cardstock. Roll the brayer in liquid polymer clay and coat the stamp. • **2.** Press the stamp on the tag firmly. Peel the tag off the stamp and bake immediately at 275° for 10 minutes. Clean the stamp right away with alcohol and then soap and water. Allow to cool.

3. Squirt a small amount of Cranberry paint on a foam square and spritz with water. Rub the pad on a scrap paper to blend the water and acrylic paint. Swipe the foam across the tag surface. The color will only adhere to the areas of the paper not coated with the baked liquid clay.

Pendants with Amazing Depth

by Judy Belcher

That same quality in metallic clay that made the 'To DYE For' Moon earrings on pages 10 - 11 sparkle makes these pendants move and dance in the light.

Instead of using a rubber stamp to create the image, try building a millefiori cane.

When manipulated just right, even the simplest of polymer clay canes come alive in your hands. Enhance a simple checkerboard or stripe with a colorful a jelly roll.

Enjoy being creative!

Pitch Black Slate Espresso Ginger Raisin Red Pepper Cranberry Terra Cotta Rust Caramel Butterscotch Latte

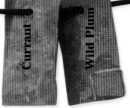
Stream · Denim · Eggplant · Currant · Wild Plum

4. Roll out a 2½" x 2½" sheet of White clay on a medium setting of the Clay Machine. Mist the stamp with water and press firmly into the clay.

5. Using the 2" and 1" circle cutters, cut out a small frame. Bake the frame at 275° for 20 minutes. Let cool.

6. Using your finger, work the Butterscotch paint into the crevices of the frame and wipe away any excess. Rebake the frame for 10 minutes to set the paint. Let cool.

7. Tape photo to frame and the frame to a slightly larger circle of Red cardstock.

8. Attach the frame to the tag and add fibers.

Gold Circle Tag
Instructions on pages 12-13

Key Tag
TIPS: Burgundy cardstock, with resist technique, colored with Posh Impressions Metallic Inkabilities - Precious Metals Kit - Silver. The key is molded from scrap polymer clay and coated with Perfect Gold and Bronze Perfect Pearls. The resin in Perfect Pearls bonds with the clay after baking.

Green Celebrate Tag
TIPS: Green cardstock with Posh Impressions Metallic Inkabilities (Precious Metals Kit - Gold; Luminous Metals Kit - Green). Translucent clay colored with Meadow and Denim Alcohol inks. Perfect Medium pen is accented with Forever Violet Perfect Pearls.

Purple and Pink Tag
TIPS: Pink cardstock, with resist technique, colored with Denim Alcohol ink. Script in Cranberry Adirondack Acrylic.

Black & Bronze Tag
TIPS: Forest Green cardstock, with resist technique, colored with Posh Impressions Metallic Inkabilities - Precious Metals Kit - Gold & Silver, accented with Black Perfect Medium pen and Bronze Perfect Pearls. The frame is scrap clay coated with Bronze Perfect Pearls, baked and antiqued with Pitch Black Alcohol Ink.

Yellow and Orange Tag
TIPS: Yellow cardstock, with resist technique, colored with Cranberry and Butterscotch Adirondack Acrylics. The letter tiles are stamped with Black Archival Ink on ecru polymer clay and edged in Cranberry and Butterscotch Alcohol Ink.

Green and Yellow Tag
TIPS: Green cardstock with resist technique, colored with Forever Violet, Green Patina and Perfect Gold Perfect Pearls. White clay embossed and colored with Archival Inks in Banana and Grape, edged with Posh Impressions Metallic Inkabilities - Precious Metals Kit - Gold.

Shell Tag
TIPS: Navy cardstock edged in Posh Impressions Metallic Inkabilities - Precious Metals Kit - Gold. The shells are molded scrap clay and coated with Blue Patina, Heirloom Gold, Green Patina and Pewter Perfect Pearls.

Pebble Mosaic
Flask

SIZE:
Flask 1¼" x 4¼" x 6" tall
Box 1¼" x 3" x 4½"
MATERIALS:
Polymer Clay:
Translucent *Kato* Polyclay
Dye Supplies:
Ranger Distress Embossing
Powders (Antique Linen, Fired
Brick, Black Soot)
Materials:
Metal Flask • 2-part Epoxy
Tools:
Clay Machine • Needle tool • Clay
blade • Non-stick Craft Sheet

Make tiny 'pebbles' of clay...

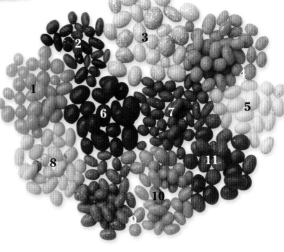

Pebble Mosaics
by Judy Belcher
Add Distress Embossing Powder to translucent clay and then roll clay into tiny pebbles. Get inspired by pebble mosaics found in books or lovely gardens.

Embossing Powder
1-Peeled Paint, 2-Black Soot, 3-Antique Linen, 4-Cement, 5-Old Paper, 6-Fired Brick/Black Soot, 7-Milled Lavender, 8-Mustard Seed, 9-Tea Dye, 10-Tattered Rose, 11-Fired Brick

1. Condition Translucent clay. • **2.** Divide the clay into 2 equal sections. Divide 1 of the sections into 3 equal parts. • **3.** Sprinkle the first sheet of clay with 1 tsp Antique Linen Distress Embossing Powder. Either knead into the clay or fold and roll through a Clay Machine. Sprinkle 1 of the smaller sheets with ½ tsp Fired Brick Distress Embossing Powder. Sprinkle the next sheet with ¼ tsp of Fired Brick and ¼ tsp of Antique Linen Distress Embossing Powder. Sprinkle the third sheet with ½ tsp of Fired Brick and a pinch of Black Soot Distress Embossing Powders. • **4.** Incorporate the distress powder into each section by rolling through Clay Machine. • **5.** Roll each section into a ⅛" diameter snake.

*Create rustic 'stone stars'
for a charming necklace, or for
great little 'starry night' dangles.*

6. Cut off small sections. • **7.** Roll into a pebble shape. Reserve some of each of the raw clay colors to make several decorative rocks for the top. • **8.** Place all the pebbles onto batting and bake at 275° for 15 minutes.

9. Store the pebbles in a compartmentalized container. • **10.** With this flask, the hinged holder of the screw on top is plastic, so twist it off. • **11.** Break the circular holder loose from the top.

12. Remove the rubber cushion inside the top for it will melt in the oven. • **13.** Wipe the flask and top with an alcohol wipe to clean it for dirt and oil residue. • **14.** Roll out light colored scrap clay on the thickest setting of the Clay Machine. Beginning on 1 side, smooth the sheet of clay across the flask to prevent air from being trapped underneath. If you see an air bubble beneath the surface, cut it with a craft knife and force the air out. Cover both sides of the flask, around the front and the top. Cut around the spout and smooth the clay around the opening. Screw on the lid tightly to mark on the clay where not to place the pebbles so the lid will still close. • **15.** Draw several simple swirl patterns with a needle tool. •**16.** Begin with the Fired Brick pebbles. Follow the design placing the pebbles very close together. Toward the end of the swirl pattern move to the lighter shades of pebbles. Following another swirl pattern, place the pebbles made with Fired Brick and Black Soot Distress Powder. Continue using various shades of the pebbles to complete all the swirl patterns.

17. Fill in the background with the pebbles made from Antique Linen Distress Powder. After the flask has been completely covered with pebbles, sprinkle the entire surface with Antique Linen distress powder. •**18.** Brush lightly with a soft bristle paintbrush to embed the distress powder around each pebble. Bake the covered flask for 30 minutes at 275°. Let cool. • **19.** Condition ½ pkg of Translucent clay and incorporate Antique Linen Distress Powder by kneading or rolling in with a Clay Machine. Use this sheet to cover the back and the bottom of the flask, taking care to avoid trapping air underneath the clay. • **20.** With the reserved clay, shape several rocks that will fit the top and stack nicely. Roll a small section on the thickest setting of the Clay Machine and form around the neck of the top. Bake the top and the flask for 20 minutes at 275°. Let cool. Remove the rocks from the top. • **21.** Scratch the metal top with the needle tool to provide a better surface to bond the rocks. Glue them to the metal with 2-part epoxy.

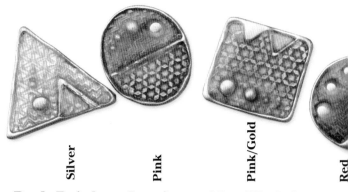

Posh Rainbow Luminous Metallic Ink on Perfect Gold Perfect Pearls

SIZE: 2" x 2"

MATERIALS:

Polymer Clay: Gold metallic clay • Liquid Polymer Clay • Scrap clay

Dye Supplies: *Ranger* (Perfect Gold Perfect Pearls; Posh Impressions Metallic Inkabilities Luminous Metallics Kit - Blue, Green, Pink; Posh Impressions Metallic Inkabilities Precious Metals Kit - Gold, Silver) • Rubber stamp • Magnet sheet • Terrifically Tacky Tape

Tools: Clay Machine • Paintbrush • Thin liner paintbrush • Toothpick • Ceramic tile • Spray bottle with water

Preparation Condition scrap clay into a sheet about as large as the rubber stamp. Before each pass through the Clay Machine, stretch the clay to release any air that might be trapped under the surface. • Roll the sheet of clay on the thickest setting of the Clay Machine. Place the sheet on a ceramic tile and firmly adhere to the tile with an acrylic rod.

1. Spray the rubber stamp with a fine mist of water. • **2.** Firmly press the stamp into the clay. • **3.** Trim the sides. Bake the mold at 275° for 30 minutes. Condition ½ pkg of Gold Clay.

Enamel Magnet
by Judy Belcher

Enameling without metalsmithing talent! The resin in the Perfect Pearls makes a lasting bond with raw clay after it is baked. By using a rubber stamp as a mold, you can make a great magnet with the fabulous depth of real enamel.

Tips & Tricks

I wanted the final magnet to look like the stamp's surface, so I made a mold of the stamp using scrap clay. Some stamps can be used just as they are, so begin with step 4.

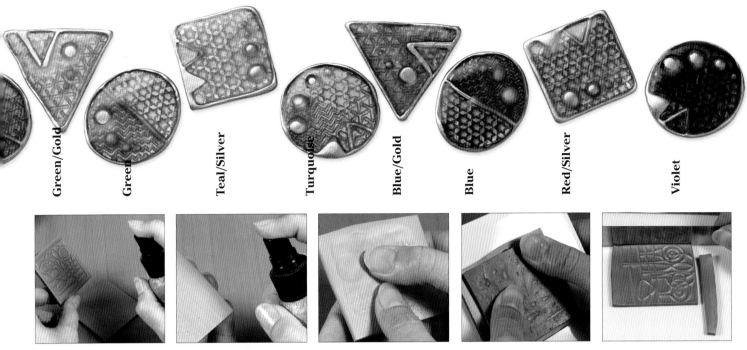

Green/Gold • Green • Teal/Silver • Turquoise • Blue/Gold • Blue • Red/Silver • Violet

4. Spray the mold with a fine mist of water. • **5.** Place the clay on the mold and spray the back of the clay with water. • **6.** Press the clay firmly into the mold with your fingers to ensure that every edge is properly formed. Allow the water to dry off the back of the clay. **7.** Place a small ceramic tile on top of the clay and press down firmly. This will smooth the back and keep the magnet from becoming distorted. Remove the mold, leaving the raw clay on the tile. • **8.** Cut away any excess clay with a clay blade, making sure to leave an edge around the sides to form the cells or cloisonne. Smooth any rough edges with your finger.

9. Brush the entire clay surface with Perfect Gold Perfect Pearls. The resins will bond with the clay during baking to form a lasting metallic shiny Gold surface on the clay. Bake the magnet on the ceramic tile for 20 minutes at 275°. • **10.** Let cool on the tile. • **11.** With a stiff dry paintbrush, brush away any loose Gold particles. • **12.** Shake the Posh Metallics before using. Pour a little at a time on a ceramic tile, then remix the ink with a paintbrush, stirring up the metallic particles. Paint the bottom of each of the cells with Inks, taking care not to cover the Gold surface of the cells. Use a thin liner paintbrush and a toothpick to spread the ink into the corners. **13.** Mix the colors for interesting effects. Paint the trees Metallic Green with a mix of Gold and Silver ink. Paint the foreground Metallic Pink with a mix of Gold ink. Posh Metallics gives the sparkly effect of opaque enamels. Let the ink dry thoroughly.

14. Fill the entire piece with liquid polymer clay. Tap the ceramic tile on your work table to force any air bubbles to the surface. • **15.** Bake for 30 minutes at 275° or until the Liquid Clay is clear. • **16.** Adhere a magnet to the back of the piece.

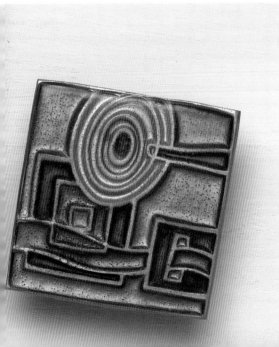

This beautiful enamel technique resembles an ancient glass and metal techniques... expensive inlaid glass colors in gold, called 'cloisonne'.

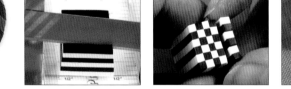

1. Condition 1 pkg each of Black and White clays. Roll out a 4" x 5" sheet of each color on the thickest setting of the Clay Machine. Cut each sheet of clay in half. • **2.** Stack 1 Black sheet of clay on a White sheet. Adhere with an acrylic rod. Cut the stack in thirds and place on top of each other. Adhere with an acrylic rod. Trim the slab so the sides are neat. • **3.** Place the striped slab cane into the Precise-A-Slice and cut 4 thin slices $1/20$" thick and set aside.

4. Turn the striped slab so you are cutting the shorter side. Cut 13 slices the same thickness as the stripe, about $1/8$" thick. • **5.** Reassemble the slices, flipping every other slice over to form a checkerboard cane. Roll each side with an acrylic rod to adhere all the slices. • **6.** Cut 4 thin slices from this cane and set aside.

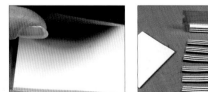
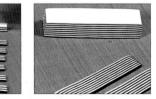

7. Stack the other 2 sheets of Black and White clay and adhere with an acrylic rod. Roll through the Clay Machine on the thickest setting. This will create thinner stripes. • **8.** Cut 3" of this sheet and set aside. With remaining sheet, repeat steps 2-6. • **9.** Cut and stack the 3" sheet from step 8 and roll through the Clay Machine for even thinner stripes. Cut several thin slices.

Reversible Bracelet
by Judy Belcher

This bracelet is made using 2 simple canes in several sizes... a striped slab and a checkerboard. Using the Adirondack Archival Inks on 1 side to color the cane makes the bracelet reversible.

In this project I use 2 of my favorite supplies: deli paper and candy paper. Deli paper is thin, unwaxed paper with a slick surface on one side. I like to use this as a working surface because I can move my project around on the table and I can peel the paper away from the clay without distorting the clay.

Candy paper is a thin clear sheet; unlike plastic wrap, it won't stick to the surface of the clay. I find this paper indispensable for removing fingerprints and it neatly adheres slices of clay together to form a sheet.

Both can be found at restaurant supply houses. The colored 'Oh' Rings add a nice dangle to the bracelet.

SIZE: 8" around
MATERIALS:
Polymer Clay: *Kato* Polyclay (Black, White)
Dye Supplies: *Ranger* Archival Ink Reinkers - Maroon, Mustard, Teal
Materials: Deli Paper • Candy Paper • Typing Paper • 42 Fancy Silver 6mm jump rings • *Fire Mountain Gems* Oh! Rings (5mm 28 each: Brick Red, Turquoise, Yellow; 7mm 14 each: Brick Red, Turquoise, Yellow; 12mm: 2 Yellow, 4 Turquoise; 15mm: 4 Brick Red, 2 Yellow) • Silver jump rings (5 of 12mm, 27 of 9mm) • Power Stretch Cord • Super glue
Tools: *Ranger* Cut N' Dry Foam • Acrylic Rod • *Val-Kat Designs* Precise-A-Slice *Ateco* cutters ($1\frac{1}{16}$" oval, 1" circle) • *Kemper* circle cutter ($\frac{1}{2}$", $\frac{5}{8}$") • *Yasatomo* Screw Punch
Bracelet Finish: Tie a Surgeons knot to complete the bracelet. 1. Right over left and around, 2. Left over right and through, 3. Through the loop again, 4. Tighten slightly, 5. Put the left over the right and through, 6. Tighten completely. Add a dab of Super glue and trim the ends.

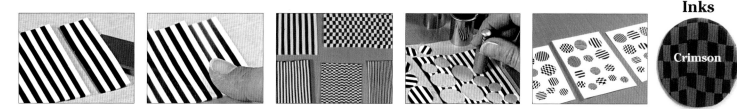

Crimson

10. Lay a sheet of deli paper on your work surface. Using the thin slices of cane from step 4, align the slices to form a stripped sheet of clay. Be sure to butt the edges firmly against each other. • 11. Place a piece of candy paper on top of the striped sheet. With your finger, gently at first and then more vigorously, rub each of the seams to adhere the slices and form a uniform sheet. Remove the clay sheet from the deli paper by gently peeling the paper away from the clay. If the clay sheet is uneven or thicker than you would like, roll it through the Clay Machine, with the stripes perpendicular to the roller. Begin on a setting as thick as your sheet and continue to thin the sheet on incrementally smaller settings until you reach #5. Lay the sheet on deli paper. Repeat steps 10-11 for each of the cane slices. • 12. You should end up with 5 different sheets of clay. A thick striped sheet, a medium striped sheet, a thin striped sheet, a larger checkerboard sheet and a smaller checkerboard sheet. 13. Using the various size cutters, cut several of each shape from each of the sheets of clay. For minimum distortion, remove the excess clay from around the shapes first and then peel the paper away from the clay disks. • 14. Lay a few of each size and pattern on 3 different sheets of typing paper. You will need at least 14 disks on each sheet, 42 total, for an 8" bracelet.

Sepia

Olive

15. Squirt a small amount of Maroon ink onto a foam square. Pat each shape firmly. This adheres the clay disk to the typing paper so the ink does not bleed onto the reverse side. Reink disk if needed. Repeat this step for the Mustard and Teal clay disks. Bake on the typing paper for 20 minutes at 275°. Let cool. While the shapes are still attached to the typing paper, wipe off any excess ink from the shapes. • 16. Place the typing paper with the shapes still attached on an old newspaper. Position the screw punch at the top of the shape and press down several times. Remove the clay disks from the typing paper.

Berry
Purple

17. Using flat-nose pliers, attach 6mm fancy Silver jump rings to all of the clay disks. 18. Attach 9mm Silver jump rings to all 15mm and 12mm Oh! Rings, 12mm Silver jump rings, and five 9mm Silver jump rings.

19. **String a Bracelet.** Cut 10" of Power Cord. Use a bead stopper, or paper clip on the end to keep your work from sliding off. String a 5mm Teal 'Oh' Ring, a 7mm Teal 'Oh' Ring, a 5mm Teal 'Oh' Ring, a Teal clay disk, a 5mm Teal 'Oh' Ring, a 7mm Teal 'Oh' Ring, a 5mm Teal 'Oh' Ring, a Silver jump ring dangle. Repeat this pattern with 6 more Teal clay disks, alternating the Silver and 'Oh' Ring dangles in every other set. When adding clay disks, make sure they are all facing either colored side up or down. This is what makes the bracelet reversible. Continue the pattern with the Mustard and Maroon disks, 'Oh' Rings and Silver dangles and then begin again with the remaining Teal, Mustard and Maroon clay disks and 'Oh' Ring and Silver dangles. Tie off bracelet.

Banana

Emerald

Cobalt

Library
Green

Additional ideas for bracelets...

Plum

Back
of
Snake

Tummy
of
Snake

Antiquities Embossing Powders

California
Stucco

Chinese Red

Terra Cotta

Rose Quartz

Tanzanite

Cobalt

Topiary

Christmas
Tree

Verdigris

Cement

Rust

Ocher

Snakes Alive

by Leslie Blackford

Make this easy life-like reptile to use as jewelry, an ornament, or just for fun.

SIZE: Large Green snake 27", Black & White stripe snake 14", Pink 18", Small Black snake 12"

MATERIALS:

Polymer Clay: *Kato* Polyclay (Black, Translucent)
Dye Supplies: *Ranger* Distress Embossing Powder - Peeled Paint, Old Paper
Materials: Seed beads
Tools: Clay Extruder

1. Condition the Translucent clay and divide in half. Mix the embossing powder with the divided Translucent clay. Roll the Translucent/embossing powder mixture into 3" long logs that are about as big around as a nickel. Roll the Black clay into the same log shape. Line the logs up side by side and cut them into discs about the same thickness as a nickel. • **2.** Restack the logs, alternating the color in a pattern. • **3.** Load the extruder with the stack of clay. • **4.** Extrude the clay.

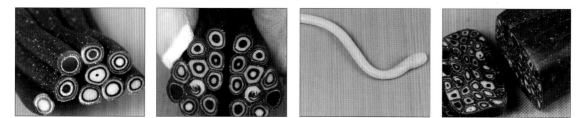

5. Cut even pieces of the extruded clay and line them up in rows of 4. • **6.** Put the rows on top of each other into a stack that is 3 rows high. • **7.** Roll out a thin log about the size of a standard pencil. Make 1 end of the log slightly smaller than the other, the thinner side being the tail and the thicker side the head. • **8.** Cut very thin slices of the extruded cane.

9. Lay them across the top of the snake. • **10.** When the length of the snake has been covered from head to tail flip the snake over and bring the ends of each cane slice together in the middle. Cut away the excess clay. **11.** Smooth the seam by gently rolling back and forth on the work surface. • **12.** Place a glass bead into each side of the head for the eyes. Bake at 270° for 15-20 minutes.

Adirondack **Embossing Powders**

Bottle

Denim

Eggplant

Cranberry

Espresso

Ginger

Butterscotch

Antique Linen   Vintage Photo   Mustard Seed   Milled Lavender   Peeled Paint   Weathered Wood

Distress Embossing Powders

Additional ideas for glow lights...

1. Coloring the clay: Wear gloves because ink will stain the skin. Condition ¼ block of Translucent clay. Roll out into a sheet on the largest setting of the Clay Machine. • **2.** Lay the sheet on waxed or parchment paper to avoid staining your work surface. Squeeze 5-10 drops of Sepia ink reinker onto the center of the clay. • **3.** Spread the ink down the middle of the clay using a cotton swab. The ink will not be dry. • **4.** Fold the sheet in half. • **5.** And in half again. Run the sheet through the Clay Machine several times using the same folding method. If the ink gets on the rollers, wipe away with a baby wipe or alcohol to avoid staining. Continue running the clay through the Clay Machine until the ink has been distributed evenly and the color is uniform.

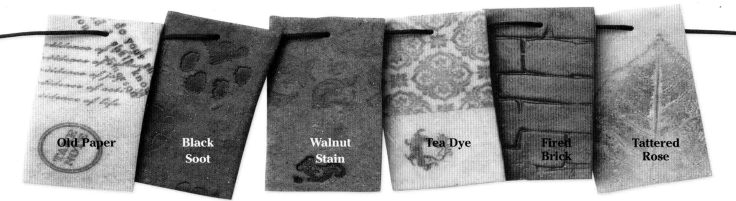

Old Paper   Black Soot   Walnut Stain   Tea Dye   Fired Brick   Tattered Rose

Distress Embossing Powders

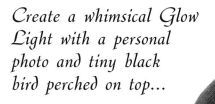

Create a whimsical Glow Light with a personal photo and tiny black bird perched on top...

Kindred Spirit Lamp
by Leslie Blackford

SIZE: 4" x 5" x 3½" deep
MATERIALS:
Polymer Clay:
Kato (Liquid Polyclay; Polyclay: 3 Translucent, 1 White)
Dye Supplies:
Ranger (Sepia Archival Ink Reinker; Weathered Wood Distress Embossing Powder; Espresso Alcohol Ink)
Materials:
3" x 4" cardboard box with lid • Black & White carbon copy of image • Clip Light with a 4-6" cord • Cotton swab • Paintbrush • Elmer's glue • Super glue
Tools:
1½" circle cutter

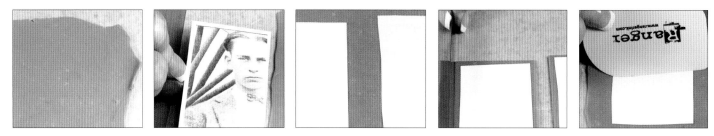

6. Image Transfer: Roll out the Sepia tinted clay on a #3 setting of the Clay Machine and lay on paper or tile. • **7.** Cut out the copy of the image for the window of the lamp. Lay the copy of the image face down onto the sheet of clay. Trim around the copy leaving ¼"-½" extra room around the image edge. Remove excess clay and set aside. • **8.** Repeat this step, making 2 copies at the same time just in case one does not come out perfectly. • **9.** Place the images and clay on the baking sheet. • **10.** Use a bone folder or the back of a spoon to brayer the image onto the clay. Make sure there are no air bubbles and that all corners are not curled up. Bake at 270° for only 10-15 minutes.

11. Once the clay has cooled off enough to handle, slowly peel the paper away from the clay. You should have an almost exact image of the copy that you selected. • **12.** The Box: Lay the transfer or a template that is the size of the image on the inside of the box lid. Trace around the image or template. • **13.** Cut out the traced line. This will frame the transfer and be the window of the box.• **14.** Outside of box: Roll out 3 ounces each of White and Translucent clay on a #1 setting. Mix about a tablespoon of Weathered Wood Distress Embossing Powder into each color separately. • **15.** Roll each clay out on a #3 setting of the Clay Machine.

16. Stack the 2 colors of clay together and roll them through the Clay Machine again. Fold the sheet in half and roll through 2 more times.
17. Cut the sheet into 1" strips and stack. We will cut slices of the stack to use as wooden planks on the outside of the box.
18.-19. Spread a very thin coat of Liquid Polymer Clay on the outside of the box lid and all 4 sides of the box. • **20.** Cut strips of the "Weathered Wood stack" and cover the entire box with the strips.

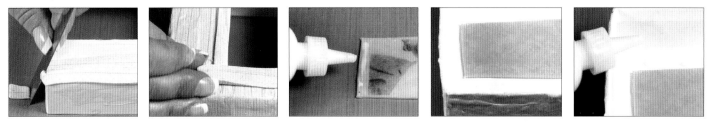

21. Trim clay even with box edge. • **22.** Add clay strips around the frame. • **23.** Picture window: Apply a thin line of glue to the edge of the image. • **24.** Lay the image on the inside of the box lid and line it up to fit into the window. • **25.** Adhere the transfer to the inside of the box.

26. Make a very slim log from the scrap clay and line the outside edge of the transfer image to secure it inside the box lid.
27-29. Add a little detail by making lines and nail holes for the wood planks. • **30.** At the bottom of the box, not the lid, mark the hole for the clip light.

31. Cut a 1½" hole in the center but more towards the back of the box. • **32.-34.** Use what is left of the stack to make 4 small blocks of clay about the size of standard dice. Adhere these on the bottom at each corner of the box. Smooth the clay around the circle hole at the bottom of the box making sure there are no rough edges. Bake the box and the lid at 275° for about 20 minutes. After the box has cooled, glue the lid onto the box. Aging: Brush on a very thin coat of Espresso ink, then wipe away the excess before it dries. • **35.** Shape and bake embellishments as desired. Adhere embellishments to the top of the box. Insert the clip light and enjoy the soft light and the memory that you have created.

1. Cut a Wonder Tape Sheet to 3⅞" x 4¾". Pop out the roller piece of Inky Roller following the package instructions. Peel off the paper backing, position and adhere sheet to Inky Roller covering it completely. Remove the Orange protective plastic from Wonder Tape Sheet on Inky Roller. Adhere lace to Roller. Re-insert roller into handle. Working over a Craft Sheet, condition and roll out enough Black clay on 6th largest setting on the Clay Machine to partially cover the journal. Using lace-covered Inky Roller, impress the lace pattern by rolling firmly over clay.

2. Tear the edge of 1 side and place clay over the book, curving and stretching clay over the edges of book. Using a NuBlade, cut excess clay from around the book along inside front cover line (the clay will be wrapped around the edges of 3 sides of cover). Rip pieces of clay from the excess and place randomly, overlapping along the jagged edge of clay. Push the cup end of ball & cup tool into a piece of Black clay that's been run through the Clay Machine on the 3rd largest setting. Pull tool out, clay will be lodged in cup. Gently press cup into overlapped clay on the book dislodging clay from the cup. Repeat until 3 buttons of clay are applied to each overlapped piece.

3. Bake clay-covered book following manufacturer's instructions. Let cool. Carefully pry clay from book. Apply a Paint Dabber to the crevices of the clay. Smear with a finger so that only a thin layer of paint remains on the clay. Let dry. Place clay back on the book and bake for 10 minutes at 265°. Let cool. Pry clay from book. Sand excess paint from surface. Scuff the wrong side of the clay with a piece of sandpaper. Glue clay in place. Tie ribbons to the binding.

Scraps of Lace Journal
by Debbie Tlach

SIZE: 5" x 7"

MATERIALS:

Polymer Clay: Black *Kato* Polyclay

Dye Supplies: *Ranger* (Willow Adirondack Acrylic Paint Dabber; Inkssentials: Inky Roller, Non-Stick Craft Sheet)

Materials: Lace scrap 3¼" x 3¾" • Ribbons • *Suze Weinberg's* Wonder Tape Sheet • 5" x 7" Kraft Book • 400 grit sandpaper • Sobo glue

Tools: Clay Machine • *Kato* NuBlade • *Ten Seconds Studio* small Ball & Cup tool

Tips and Techniques

1. Use various colors of *Adirondack* Acrylic Paint Dabbers on the same piece. Try using coordinating colors for a subtle monochromatic look.

2. Use Metallic Inkabilities in place of the Adirondack Acrylic Paint Dabbers for a slightly metallic look.

3. Adhere textured fabric, netting or Pop it! Shapes onto a roller to create custom textures. Carve into a roller to create an entire arsenal of patterns for infinite possibilities. Inky rollers and extra rollers are available in 3 sizes. Adorn several replacement rollers for a variety of textures.

TIP: Use the same technique to make a coordinating bookmark.

Coffee · Sepia · Russet · Crimson · Tangerine · Banana · Mustard · Olive · Emerald · Aqua

Archival Ink & Archival Brights Reinkers

Creative Character Sun Lamp

by Leslie Blackford

The use of translucent polymer clay mixed with Ranger Archival ink adds a luminous glow and a sense of mystery to my creations.

Flying Pig:

SIZE: ¾" x 2" x 1½" long

INSTRUCTIONS: Use a bit of leftover cloud clay to sculpt the wings. Shape the pig from clay mixed with California Stucco Antiquities Embossing Powder. Use a dot of Black clay to form the eyes and tips of the feet. Poke a small hole in the underside of the pig using a needle tool. Bake following manufacturer's instructions. Adhere wings to pig. Adhere wire to hole in underside. Wrap other end of wire around a sunbeam.

SIZE:
Sun 4½" diameter, 7½" tall
Box 4¼" x 4⅜" x 3" deep

MATERIALS:
Polymer Clay: *Kato* (Liquid Polyclay; Polyclay: Black, Blue, Green, Yellow, Translucent, White)
Dye Supplies: *Ranger* (Tangerine Archival Ink Reinker; California Stucco Antiquities Powder; Adirondack Alcohol Inks - Red Pepper, Denim)
Materials: 3" x 5" or 3" x 3" glass globe the size of *Glade* Candle Globes • Clip light • 2 Clear craft marbles • A few seed beads • Small piece of spring wire • Rubber gloves • Cotton swab • Super glue
Tools: Clay Machine • 1½ " circle cutter • 3" round cutter • Sculpting tool

1. Prepare the clay: Wear rubber gloves because the ink will stain your hands. Condition ½ of a large block of Translucent clay and roll out on a #1 setting of the Clay Machine. Squeeze out 10-20 drops of Tangerine ink onto the center of the sheet of clay. Spread it around the center using a cotton swab. Fold in half and then in half again. Roll through the Clay Machine several times until the clay and the ink have mixed together evenly. • **2.** Covering the globe: Roll out the clay on a #3 setting of the Clay Machine. Set the glass globe upside down on your work surface. Lay the sheet of clay over the glass globe. • **3.** Gently bring the excess clay together at one place on the globe. • **4.** Cut away the excess. • **5.** Trim away the clay hanging over the bottom of the globe. Smooth out marks and fingerprints.

Library Green • True Blue • Teal • Berry Purple • Cobalt • Grape • Jet Black • Plum • Maroon • Carnation

Archival Ink & Archival Brights Reinkers

6. Eyes: Condition a small piece of Yellow, Green, and Black clay. Roll each out on a #1 setting of the Clay Machine. • **7.** Make a stack with the Green, Yellow and Black, alternating the colors. Cut the stack long ways into thirds. • **8.** Pinch together 1 end of each piece into a point making a long triangle shape. • **9.** Make a small log shape from the Black clay. Place the small end of the triangle pieces all around the log of Black clay. Roll slightly making sure there is no air trapped inside. Cut 2 thin even slices. • **10.** Put a very tiny drop of Liquid Polyclay onto the flat side of a craft marble. Place the slices of the "iris cane" onto the drop of Liquid Polyclay. Look through the other side of the marble to see how the eye will appear. Manipulate the clay so that both eyes look alike and make sure there are no air bubbles inside the eye. Bake at 275° for 10 minutes.

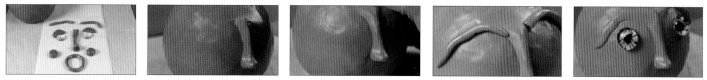

11. Sculpt Face: Shape a small piece of clay into a triangle for the nose. • **12.** Center nose onto the face. • **13.** Smooth out seams of the nose. • **14.** Roll out a log the size of a pencil. Cut log in half. Position eyebrows and smooth. • **15.** Set the eyes on the face.

16. Roll out a log about the size of a pencil. Cut the log in half. Put the 2 pieces of the logs on top of each other to form the lips. Place the lips under the nose. • **17.** Make two marble sized balls of the clay and cut in half. Place a ball at each end of the lips with the flat side against the face. Make an indention with a needle tool at the point where the half circle and the corner of the lips meet to create a smile. **18.** Place another half ball for the chin. • **19.** Make a cookie shape from some of the extra clay and cut it in half. Place each one about 1/3 of the way over each eye. Smooth the edges. • **20.** Manipulate the eyelid until you like the look. The eyes make all the difference in a face. Lifting the lid upward at the center of the eye will give the face a softer expression. Optional: After baking, apply Red Pepper Alcohol Ink with a cotton swab to the lips and eyelids.

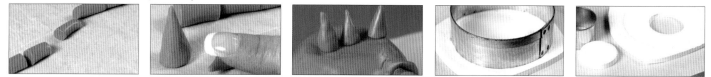

21. Sunbeams: Make a log about a foot long and about the size of a first grade pencil. Cut the log into 3/4"-1" pieces. • **22.** Shape each piece into a cone. • **23.** Put a very tiny dot of Liquid Polyclay on the flat end of the cones and center them around the sides of the sun. Make sure all of the cones are attached firmly. Smooth out any marks or indentations in the clay. Bake the globe at 275° for 20 minutes. Allow to cool completely before removing from the oven. • **24.** Lamp base: Roll out a block of White clay on the #1 setting. Fold the sheet in half so that you have a double thickness of the #1 setting. Place the globe upside down onto the sheet of clay and press lightly to leave an indention of the mouth of the globe. Cut out the base. • **25.** Cut about 1/2" beyond the indention that was left by the globe. Cut away the excess. Use a 1" circle cutter to cut out a hole in the center of the circular indention. This will be the hole for the clip light.

26. Place a small line of Liquid Polyclay in the indention that the was left by the globe. • **27.** Place globe back into the place where indention was made. Bake at 275° for 15 minutes and allow to cool in oven. • **28.** Wrap the edges of white bottom around base of sun face.
29. Clouds: Condition about half a block each of White and Translucent clays. Squeeze 15 drops of Denim ink onto each clay. Spread ink with a cotton swab. Allow 10 minutes to dry. Marble the colors together and make irregular cloud shapes. Apply a thin coat of Liquid Polyclay to the bottom of the face. Randomly place the clouds around the bottom of the sun. Use leftover clay to form 4 feet 5/8" x 1 1/2" x 1/2" tall. Bake again at 275° for 20 minutes. Allow to cool completely before removing from the oven. • **30.** Adhere feet to the bottom of the lamp with Super glue. Insert the clip light.

Pearlized Opener and Pen

by Kim Cavender

There are many ways of doing 'Mokume Gane' with polymer clay and here's one more to add to the list. Use mica powders to tint Translucent clay, the results are a soft, muted effect with a lovely pearl sheen.

SIZE: Pen 6"
Letter opener handle 4"
Wine cork 1½" diameter

MATERIALS:

Polymer Clay: *Kato* Polyclay (Translucent, White)

Dye Supplies: *Ranger* (*Perfect Pearls* pigment powders - Perfect Gold, Turquoise, Forever Green, Forever Violet, Berry Twist)

Materials: Purchased letter opener with a wooden or metal handle • Paper Mate Comfort Mate ink pen • Wet/dry sandpaper (400, 600. 800 grit) • Sobo glue

Tools: Clay Machine • *Kato* Ripple blade • Clay blade • Large knitting needle or brayer • Buffing wheel or polymer compatible gloss varnish

Pearlized handles have a gorgeous look of elegance and a smooth, touchable texture.

1. Remove the ink cartridge from the pen. Coat the barrel of the pen and the handle of the letter opener with a thin coat of Sobo glue to help the clay adhere to the pieces during baking. • **2.** Cut the block of Translucent clay into 5 equal pieces. Condition each piece and mix each with a different color of the Pearl powder. Add a little at a time, folding the clay in half, and pinching the edges closed before running it through the Clay Machine. • **3.** Roll each sheet to the 4th largest setting on your Clay Machine. Stack the sheets in the following order: Turquoise, Gold, Green, Berry, and Violet. • **4.** Cut the stack in half and stack again. Repeat 2 more times. • **5.** Use the wavy blade to cut down into the stack, making both vertical and horizontal cuts very close together. Gently press the stack back together.

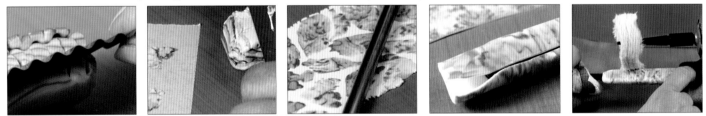

6. Turn the stack on its side and cut again, holding the blade parallel to the layers of clay. Press the stack gently back together and turn it back over onto your work surface. **7.** Use the regular clay blade to slice very thin pieces from the surface of the stack. Lay these pieces onto a sheet of parchment paper. • **8.** Condition ¼ block of White clay at the 4th largest setting on your Clay Machine. Begin placing the slices from the block onto the White clay, taking care not to overlap them. Roll them smoothly into place with a large knitting needle or brayer. Continue to add slices cut from the Mokume stack to fill in all the empty areas on the sheet. Roll each layer into place. Slide your clay blade under the patterned sheet to loosen it from your work surface and run it through the Clay Machine on the 4th largest setting to ensure that all your layers are smooth. • **9.** Wrap the sheet around the letter opener, trimming away the excess clay to use for covering the ink pen. Smooth the seam carefully and add very thin slices to help hide the seam. Use the knitting needle to smooth them into place. Cover the ink pen barrel the same way. Bake both pieces at 275° for 30 minutes. If your letter opener has a wooden handle, let it cool in the oven to avoid cracking. • **10.** Sand the pieces with the 400, 600, and 800 grit wet/dry sandpaper in a small bowl of water to which you've added a drop of dishwashing liquid. Rinse the pieces well and dry them. Buff them on a muslin buffing wheel using a heavy potholder over the sharp metal blade of the letter opener. If desired, coat the pieces with a polymer compatible gloss varnish. Reassemble the ink pen.

'Captured Stone' Pendant

by Kim Cavender

Rocks are one of my passions. I have a hard time passing by an interesting specimen without stopping to pick it up to add to my collection.

Distress Embossing Powders make it easy to get realistic stone effects using Translucent polymer clay. The added contrast of faux hammered metal adds a great ancient touch.

SIZE:
Leaf pendant 1" x 3"
Banded pendant 1" x 2⅜"

MATERIALS:

Polymer Clay:
Kato (Liquid Polyclay; Polyclay: Translucent, Black)

Dye Supplies:
Ranger (*Perfect Pearls* Aged Patina kit; *Distress Embossing Powders* - Vintage Photo, Tea Dye, Walnut Stain, Black Soot, Peeled Paint)

Materials:
Jewelry cord or necklace wire • Small twig or leaf

Tools:
Clay Machine • Clay blade • Soft brush • Large ball stylus • Smoothing tool or needle tool • Wet/dry sandpaper (400 and 600 grit)

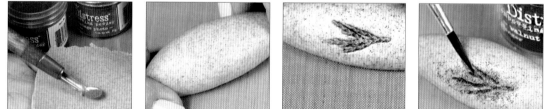

1. Condition ⅓ pkg Translucent clay. Add small amounts of Distress Powders until clay acquires a variegated stone-look. • **2.** Shape clay into an oval using your fingers to draw out the ends to refine the shape. Flatten the pendant shape slightly against work surface. • **3.** Press a small twig or leaf into the pendant. Remove the twig and set aside. • **4.** With a small brush, apply a bit of Walnut Stain Distress Powder into the twig impression. Excess powder that sticks to the pendant can be sanded off after baking. With your finger, apply dabs of Distress Powder around the pendant. Bake the pendant at 275° for 30 minutes. Let cool. Sand the pendant with wet/dry sandpaper to remove any excess powder and to smooth the surface.

5. Condition a small amount of Black clay on the 5th largest setting of the Clay Machine. Brush a little Liquid Polyclay on 1 end of the pendant. Wrap the Black clay around it to form an end cap. Use the small brush to apply the powders in the Aged Patina set. Use the ball stylus to texture the Black clay to get the look of hammered metal. Cut away any excess clay and touch up as needed with powders. Repeat this step for the other end of the pendant. • **6.** Cut a small strip of Black clay from clay run through the Clay Machine on the 4th setting. This should be as wide as you would like the bail of your pendant to be. Texture the piece lightly with the ball stylus. Use the Pearl powders to add the aged patina. • **7.** Wrap it into a bail shape. Adhere it to the top of the pendant with a drop of Liquid Polyclay. Using a smoothing tool, make sure the bail is adhered well to the top of the pendant. Retexture and apply more Pearl powders if needed. **8.** Roll a thin snake of Black clay and attach it to your pendant by brushing on a drop or two of Liquid Polyclay. Bake the pendant again at 275° for 30 minutes. Let cool and string onto jewelry cord or wire.

Use these techniques on a larger scale to make a coordinating purse.

Caning with Embossing Powders

By Kim Cavender

I recently took part in a design challenge which involved decorating using Ranger products in combination with clay. I wasn't sure what direction I wanted to go until I tried Adirondack embossing powders.

I had never seen canework done using only the powders to tint Translucent clay. I am thrilled with the outcome and I'm excited to share the possibilities.

Embossing Powder Tips

Adding embossing powders to clay can be messy but the results are well worth the effort. Adding small amounts at a time, folding the clay in half, and pinching the sides closed before running it through the Clay Machine will make it a little easier.

As a general guideline, a half pkg of clay to ½ tsp. of embossing powder seems about right. Try a little more or less depending on the effect you're after. Adding too much of the powder can compromise the strength of the clay. I've found that the chunkier powders should be used a bit more sparingly than the fine ones.

Ocean Dreams Mini Clutch

by Kim Cavender

The inspiration for this design came from an afternoon spent snorkeling off the coast of Belize. The water was an amazing shade of aqua. It's a breeze to duplicate this color and many others by mixing Translucent clay with embossing powders. Use this mini clutch to hold cash and credit cards for a quick shopping trip or a night out on the town.

SIZE: 3" x 5¼" x 1" tall

MATERIALS:

Polymer Clay: *Kato* Polyclay (Translucent, Black, White)
Supplies: *Ranger* (Rubit Scrubit pad to texture clay; *Adirondack* Embossing Powders - Denim, Bottle, Butterscotch, Ginger)
Materials: Large metal cigarette case • 2 part epoxy or another glue suitable for bonding clay to metal
Tools: Clay Machine • Clay blade • Knitting needle or brayer

Ocean Dreams Key Ring

by Kim Cavender

Make a coordinating secret compartment key ring using the leftover pieces of clay from your clutch purse. You can find these key rings online at www.polymerclayprojects.com.

SIZE: 3¼" long, ½" diameter

MATERIALS:

Supplies: Metal cylinder key ring • Refer to Mini Clutch Purse

INSTRUCTIONS:

1. Mix the scrap pieces from your Skinner blend and roll them through the Clay Machine at a #4 setting. Wrap this sheet around the brass tube that comes with the key ring and cut the clay at the point where the edges overlap. Remove the excess clay and smooth the seam together. Texture the tube with the Rubit Scrubit pad and trim away the excess clay from both ends.
2. Decorate the tube with little Black tapered strips and tiny cane slices. Bake at 275° for 30 minutes and let cool. Assemble the key ring.

1. Cut the bar of Translucent clay into thirds and set 1 aside. To 1 piece, add the Ginger embossing powder a little at a time until you have a nice Sandy color. Mix the Denim and Bottle colors together into another piece to make an Aqua color. Roll the Sand and Aqua pieces separately through the Clay Machine at the thickest setting and form 2 rectangles. • **2.** Cut each rectangle diagonally from corner to corner and stack the resulting triangles. • **3.** Arrange the triangles to form another rectangle with the corners offset. Cut off the corners and press lightly so the triangles stick together. • **4.** With both colors touching the rollers, roll the clay at the thickest setting. Fold the sheet in half, with the same color edges lined up. Roll through the Clay Machine fold-first. Repeat folding and rolling the clay through the Clay Machine until the clay is completely blended from sand to aqua. With both colors touching the rollers, run the blended sheet of clay through the Clay Machine on the second largest setting without folding it. Continue to run the clay through the Clay Machine thinning it to the fourth largest setting. • **5.** Cut the sheet of clay in half and place one piece on the lid of the metal case. Smooth it carefully into place, taking care not to trap air bubbles under the clay. Use the clay blade to trim the excess clay from the lid, making sure the hinges are left uncovered.

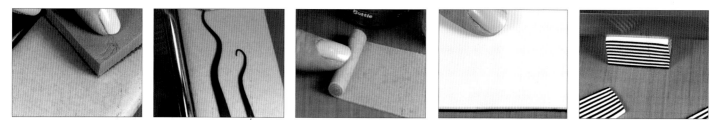

6. Texture the sides and the top of the lid by impressing the Rubit Scrubit pad into the clay. Trim again if necessary. • **7.** Condition a piece of Black clay at a very thin setting on the Clay Machine. Use a clay blade to cut tapered strips to place on the lid. Curve them into place and press gently to adhere. • **8.** Using the remaining section of Translucent clay, mix together Bottle and Butterscotch colors to make Lime Green clay. Roll this sheet up into a log approximately 1½" tall and 1" diameter. Set this piece aside. • **9.** Condition a piece of the Black and White clays at the 5th largest setting on the Clay Machine. Place the White sheet on top of Black, smoothing it into place to avoid trapping air bubbles. • **10.** Cut this rectangle in half and stack again to make a stack with 4 alternating layers. Cut the block in half and stack 2 more times. Use a clay blade to trim away uneven edges. Cut several thin slices from the side of block and set aside.

11. Roll a thin piece of Black clay about 2" wide x 4" long. Lay slices from the striped stack side by side, making sure the Black and White stripes are always alternating. Roll over them lightly with a knitting needle or brayer to adhere them together. Slide your clay blade under this sheet and run it through the Clay Machine with the stripes running vertically until you reach the 4th largest setting. • **12.** Wrap this sheet of striped clay around the Lime Green log of clay, carefully trimming away the excess. Smooth and roll the clay to adhere the seam. Reduce the cane by pinching the ends and gently rolling and stretching it. Work slowly to prevent the stripes from twisting. Reduce to a diameter of ³⁄₁₆". • **13.** Cut thin slices from the cane and arrange them on the lid of the case. Press gently to adhere them. Bake the case at 275° for 30 minutes. Let it cool. Decorate and bake the other side of the case the same way. Let cool. Carefully pry the clay away from the metal case and use a 2-part epoxy to permanently attach both pieces to the case. • **14.** Use leftover scraps of clay to cover a key ring.

Imagine Tag ATC

SIZE: 2½" x 3½"
MATERIALS:
Polymer Clay:
White *Kato* Polyclay
Supplies:
Ranger (Archival Ink Reinkers - Carnation, True Blue, Emerald, Banana, Crimson; Jet Black Archival Ink pad)
Materials:
Rubber stamp (*Invoke Arts* Imagine tag)

Passion ATC

SIZE: 2½" x 3½"
MATERIALS:
Polymer Clay: Translucent *Kato* Polyclay mixed with *Ranger* Antique Linen Distress Powder
Supplies: *Ranger* (Archival Ink Reinkers - Sepia, Aqua, Crimson; Jet Black Archival Ink pad)
Materials: Rubber stamps (*Invoke Arts* Sweet Tweet, Honey bee, Collage words I, Textures II)

Venus ATC

SIZE: 2½" x 3½"
MATERIALS:
Polymer Clay: White *Kato* Polyclay
Supplies: *Ranger* (Rustic Lodge Adirondack Alcohol Ink Kit; Adirondack Blending Solution; Adirondack Pigment Pens - Lettuce, Stream; Archival Ink pads - Jet Black, Coffee)
Materials: Rubber stamps (*Invoke Arts* Venus tag, Artpost I) • Small *Swarovski* crystal • *Fire Mountain Gems* Oh! Rings (Yellow, Rust)

Game Pieces ATC

SIZE: 2½" x 3½"
MATERIALS:
Polymer Clay: Translucent *Kato* Polyclay mixed with *Ranger* Fired Brick Distress Powder
Supplies: *Ranger* Jet Black Archival Ink pad
Materials: Rubber stamp (*Invoke Arts* Game pieces)

Polymer Clay ATC's

by Kim Cavender

I was first introduced to ATC's by my friend Cathy Johnston and I've been hooked ever since. These polymer clay versions are fun to make and surprisingly durable. The possibilities for inclusions and surface treatments are limited only by your imagination.

I start by cutting a template from quilter's plastic as a guideline to use in creating my cards. This helps me to know exactly where to stamp my cards. I prefer to do the final cutting after the cards are baked so I can get crisp, clean lines. I also like to round the edges with a corner punch after the cards have been cut.

ATC's are always 2½" x 3½" in size. It's best to start with a sheet of clay about 3" x 4", rolled to the 6th thickest setting on the Clay Machine. I bake mine on a ceramic tile that's been covered with parchment paper. After baking, I lay another parchment covered tile face down on the cards to keep them flat as they cool.

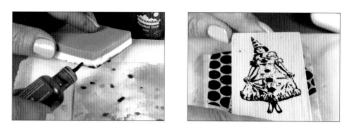

1. Place a piece of White clay on the parchment-covered tile and lightly texture both sides with the Rubit Scrubit pad. Apply small drops of Slate, Meadow, and Currant inks to the clay. Add small drops of Alcohol Blending Solution until you like the effect. Let the ink dry. Turn the clay over and apply inks to the back of the clay also. **2.** Use Black ink pad to stamp the image and phrase onto the clay. Use Plum ink to stamp polka dots. Press only hard enough to transfer ink but not hard enough to make an impression in the clay. Bake on the ceramic tile at 275° for 30 minutes. Cover with parchment paper and another ceramic tile. Let cool.

3. Use the guillotine trimmer to cut the card to 2½" x 3½".
4. Round the edges of the card using the corner punch. Use the marker to draw a swirly design on the card.

Discovery Tag ATC

SIZE: 2½" x 3½"
MATERIALS:
Polymer Clay: Translucent *Kato* Polyclay mixed with *Ranger* Mustard Seed Distress Powder
Supplies: *Ranger* (Perfect Gold Perfect Pearls Powder; Tangerine Archival Ink Reinker; Archival Jet Black Ink pad)
Materials: Rubber stamps (*Invoke Arts* Discovery tag, Textures II)

Poceline Clown ATC

SIZE: 2½" x 3½"
MATERIALS:
Polymer Clay: White *Kato* Polyclay
Supplies: *Ranger* (Adirondack Alcohol Blending Solution; Lettuce Adirondack Pigment Pen; Plum Archival Ink Reinker; Jet Black Archival Ink pad; Adirondack Cottage Path Alcohol Ink set - Slate, Meadow, Currant)
Materials: Rubber stamps (*Invoke Arts* Small Poceline, Art-phrases II, Textures II) • 2 small ceramic tiles • Parchment paper
Tools: Clay Machine • Clay blade • *Ranger* Rubit Scrubit pad • *Tonic Studios* (12" guillotine, Corner punch)

Inspire ATC

SIZE: 2½" x 3½"
MATERIALS:
Polymer Clay: Translucent *Kato* Polyclay mixed with *Ranger* Peeled Paint Distress Powder
Supplies: *Ranger* (Olive Archival Ink Reinker; Archival Ink pads Jet Black, Crimson)
Materials: Rubber stamps (*Invoke Arts* Dream face blocks, Textures II, Artwords I)

Judy Belcher

Judy's art has been juried into national exhibitions and is sold through galleries across the country. She is author of the book Polymer Clay Creative Traditions. Judy is a frequent guest artist for the Carol Duvall Show (HGTV, DIY) and for Beads, Baubles and Jewels (PBS).

www.judybelcherdesigns.com

Kim Cavender

Kim is a full-time polymer clay artist who firmly believes that Lime Green is the new neutral. She travels frequently to teach the exciting medium of polymer clay at workshops and trade shows. She is a guest of The Carol Duvall Show (HGTV) and author of Polymer Clay for the Fun of It.

www.kimcavender.com.

Leslie Blackford

Leslie's unique, primitive style distinguishes her sculptural polymer clay art. Recently published in 3 books, she travels across the country teaching workshops.

Donna Kato

Donna is a well known polymer clay artist and teacher. Her work in polymer clay is innovative, colorful and outstanding. She has appeared on The Carol Duvall Show and numerous other television shows as well.

www.katopolyclay.com

Debbie Tlach

Debbie has a background in fine arts and has been working at Ranger Industries for over 12 years. She works fearlessly in many mediums and encourages others to do so.

Speckled Spike Necklace

by Kim Cavender

These delightfully bright and speckled beads are a breeze to make using Ultra Thick Embossing Enamels and Translucent clay.

I have found that some brands of clay react differently with embossing powders. Your results may vary with other clay brands. It's important not to use more than the recommended amount of embossing powder.

SIZE:
Long Green pendant ½" x 2½"
Blue pendant ½" x 2"
Short Green pendant ½" x 1"

MATERIALS:
Polymer Clay: Translucent *Kato* Polyclay
Supplies: *Ranger* (UTEE Brightz - Blue Iris, Green Zinnia, Violet)
Materials: 4 Silver spacer beads • 1/16" diameter Black rubber necklace cord • #5 o-ring • Super glue
Tools: Clay Machine • Clay blade • Measuring spoons • 2" circle cutter • Needle tool or bamboo skewer • Wet/dry sandpaper (320, 400, 600 grit) • Buffing wheel or polymer clay compatible gloss varnish